CRYPTS, TOMBS, AND SECRET ROOMS

RUSSIA'S
CITY OF THE DEAD

BY ENZO GEORGE

Gareth Stevens
PUBLISHING

Please visit our website, www.garethstevens.com. For a free color catalog of all our high-quality books, call toll free 1-800-542-2595 or fax 1-877-542-2596.

Cataloging-in-Publication Data
Names: George, Enzo.
Title: Russia's city of the dead / Enzo George.
Description: New York : Gareth Stevens Publishing, 2018. | Series: Crypts, tombs, and secret rooms |
    Includes index.
Identifiers: ISBN 9781538206621 (pbk.) | ISBN 9781538206560 (library bound) |
    ISBN 9781538206447 (6 pack)
Subjects: LCSH: Caucasus--Social life and customs. | Caucasus--Civilization. | Russia (Federation).
Classification: LCC DK509.G47 2018 | DDC 947.5--dc23

Published in 2018 by
Gareth Stevens Publishing
111 East 14th Street, Suite 349
New York, NY 10003

For Brown Bear Books Ltd:
Managing Editor: Tim Cooke
Designer: Lynne Lennon
Editorial Director: Lindsey Lowe
Children's Publisher: Anne O'Daly
Design Manager: Keith Davis
Picture Manager: Sophie Mortimer

Picture credits:
Cover: Patrick Horton
Interior: 123rf: Olena Komyeyeva 35, Svetlana Yudina 7; **Departmen of Defense:** 40; **Dreamstime:** 19,
25, Dmitri Monastyrski 36, Vadim Rodnev 16, Nikolau Sokolovskyi 39, Lucie Zmova 38; **Public Domain:** 21,
26, 29, 33, Bibliothéque Nationale de France/Barry Capitaine 23, Le Musée absolu, Phaidon 17, Oleg Moro
13, 31, 32, Vsia Osetia 42, Radio Lemberg/ua/Yanish E 14, Rartat 12, State Historical Museum, Moscow/
lj.rossia.org 20, Alex Svirkin 8, 10, 24, 30, Tehran Museum of Contemporary Art 22, Tretyakov Gallery,
Moscow 18; **Shutterstock:** 9, 28, Igor Golovniov 37, Tanya Grudko 34, Oleg Kharkhan 15, Valery Kraynov
5, Pecold 41, Nastya Tepikina 11; **Thinkstock:** Dorling Kindersley 27, istockphoto 6 43.

All other images Brown Bear Books

Brown Bear Books has made every attempt to contact the copyright holder.
If anyone has any information please contact licensing@brownbearbooks.co.uk

Printed in the United States of America
CPSIA compliance information: Batch CS17GS: For further information contact Gareth Stevens, New York, New York at 1-800-542-2595.

CONTENTS

WORDS IN THE GLOSSARY APPEAR IN **BOLD** TYPE
THE FIRST TIME THEY ARE USED IN THE TEXT.

HOUSES ON THE HILL

Deep in the mountains of the Russian **republic** of North Ossetia is a mysterious city. There are nearly 100 buildings, but nobody lives there. The distinctive huts have tall, triangular roofs, a little like large beehives. They might be around 500 years old — or they might be far older. The site is known as the "City of the Dead."

Inside the huts are the remains of up to 10,000 people. Some bodies have been **mummified** by the cold, dry weather. Other remains are little more than scattered bones. Experts believe that some of the people were placed in the huts when they were still alive. Today, almost nobody visits the houses on the hillside. The location is difficult to reach and regional politics has led to terrorist attacks. That prevents tourists or **archaeologists** from visiting the site. Experts therefore know little about the origins of the city and the people who built it — or why they built it.

The huts stand on a remote hill in the Caucasus Mountains. The pointed roofs make them resemble beehives.

STONES OF THE PAST

The City of the Dead spreads over a 10.5-mile (17 km) mountain valley outside the village of Dargavs in the southeastern part of the Russian republic of North Ossetia. North Ossetia lies in the Caucasus region, which is dominated by the towering snow-capped Caucasus Mountains. Much of North Ossetia is made up of steep mountains and dense forests.

Some of the smaller huts have flat roofs. They may have been built by poorer people.

The valley of the City of the Dead lies in a remote part of the country. The Gizeldon River flows through the valley. The largest concentration of buildings has nearly 100 abandoned huts of different sizes. They cling to the side of a hill surrounded by a low stone wall. At the top of the hill stands a stone watchtower.

STRANGE CONSTRUCTIONS

Many of the stone huts have pointed roofs, like large beehives. Most are small, single-room dwellings, but some of the buildings farther up the hill are taller. The builders used lime-clay or lime **mortar** to cement the stone blocks together. The huts all have a small doorway on one side.

The taller huts also have a higher small square window on one side. Experts believe these holes might have been used to pass **corpses** through into the houses.

The smaller buildings are one story high and rectangular. Their roofs have a shallow **pitch**. Other huts have steep-pitched roofs made from ledges of stacked slates. The ledges protrude out from the sides of the roof. Other roofs are made from layers of stone stacked inward until the four sides meet in a peak. Some tall huts have a pointed stone on the top.

WHAT'S INSIDE?

Inside the huts, human bones and skulls are jumbled up together. In some huts, parts of bodies have become mummified, meaning they have been dried out and preserved.

The layers of slates on this roof become smaller as they rise higher. A small upright stone forms a point at the top.

The Caucasus Mountains form a barrier across the narrow strip of land between the Black and Caspian Seas.

THE CAUCASUS MOUNTAINS

THE CAUCASUS MOUNTAINS ARE TWO PARALLEL MOUNTAIN RANGES IN CENTRAL ASIA. THEY RUN FOR MORE THAN 600 MILES (1,000 KM) BETWEEN THE BLACK SEA IN THE WEST AND THE CASPIAN SEA IN THE EAST. THE HIGHEST PEAK IS MOUNT ELBRUS. NORTH OSSETIA IS PART OF RUSSIA, WHICH IS CONSIDERED TO BE PART OF EUROPE, SO AT 18,510 FEET (5,642 M), MOUNT ELBRUS IS THE HIGHEST PEAK IN EUROPE. THE CITY OF THE DEAD LIES IN THE FOOTHILLS OF THE LESSER CAUCASUS RANGE. THIS RANGE LIES 62 MILES (100 KM) SOUTH OF THE GREATER CAUCASUS RANGE. THE BUILDERS OF THE CITY LIVED IN THE RIVER VALLEYS AND PLAINS OF THE FOOTHILLS. WINTERS IN THE CAUCASUS ARE HARSH, WITH HEAVY SNOWFALL.

The small doorways in front of the huts do not have doors in them. The huts are left open to the elements.

Some of the bones lie in wooden boats inside the huts. According to some sources, early explorers found items such as weapons and clothing, but archaeologists today cannot confirm that this is true.

Experts believe that each hut was used as a **crypt** for a family living in the valley. The larger and wealthier the family, the taller the crypt they built. Experts also think that the builders dug underground crypts into the mountainside, but those crypts have not been **excavated**. There is also what seems to be a common crypt. This was likely used for strangers and those villagers who had no family to bury them.

UNIQUE ROOFS

THE BUILDINGS AT DARGAVS HAVE ROOFS LINED WITH RIDGES OF SLATE. THIS FEATURE IS FOUND IN THE BUILDINGS OF THE NAKH. THE NAKH WERE AN ANCIENT PEOPLE WHO MOVED TO THE CAUCASUS REGION FROM THE MIDDLE EAST IN AROUND 10,000 BC. THEY WERE THE ANCESTORS OF THE ALANS, WHO WERE IN TURN THE ANCESTORS OF THE OSSETIANS. THE PITCHED SLATE ROOFS WERE FIRST USED BY THE NAKH. THEY APPEAR IN NAKH BUILDINGS THROUGHOUT THE CAUCASUS.

The narrow edges of slate on some of the roofs may reflect the influence of Nakh architecture on whoever built the City of the Dead.

11

Human remains are scattered inside the huts. Some bodies are well preserved. Others are just odd bones.

Farther up the hill is a single stone tower. The top part of the tower is missing. The tower looks down on the beehive huts and across the valley toward the snow-capped mountains.

THE STONE TOWER

Historians cannot say for sure what the huts were used for, or when the people inside died. Some experts think the huts date back to the 1100s. Others believe the huts were built more recently, in the 1500s. According to one local story, the last hut was not constructed until 1830.

Another mystery is whether the people were put in the huts when they were dead, or while they were still alive. The mummified remains in some huts suggest they must have been put there after the person had died. But local legends say that people were still alive when they entered the huts.

SKILLED BUILDERS

THE HUTS AT DARGAVS WERE BUILT BY PEOPLE WITH ADVANCED CONSTRUCTION SKILLS. SOME OF THE TALLER HUTS ARE TWO TO FOUR STORIES HIGH. THEY USE PYRAMID-SHAPED **GROIN VAULTS** TO HOLD UP THE ROOF. THE ROMANS FIRST DEVELOPED THE GROIN VAULT. A GROIN VAULT IS MADE BY INTERSECTING TWO BARREL VAULTS AT RIGHT ANGLES. THE BUILDERS HAD TO BE SKILLED TO ALIGN THE STONES SO THAT THE ROOF HELD UP.

The tower looks over the whole site. There is no way to tell if it had a practical purpose, or if it was symbolic.

WHO BUILT THE MONUMENT?

Experts are not sure who built the mysterious City of the Dead. Could it have been the Alan people who once lived in the region? The Alans were a **nomadic** tribe who originated in what is now Iran. Nearly 2,000 years ago, they moved west from Iran into the Caucasus. They are said to be the ancestors of the present-day Ossetians. The Alans set up a kingdom named Alania on the plains west of the Caucasus Mountains.

Archaeologists could find out lots of information about the people in the huts if they had access to the remains.

THE DARIAL PASS

ALANIA GUARDED AN IMPORTANT PASS THROUGH THE CAUCASUS MOUNTAINS. THE DARIAL PASS TAKES ITS NAME FROM THE PERSIAN FOR "GATES OF ALAN." THE ALANS' TERRITORY LAY TO THE NORTH OF THE PASS. LEGEND SAYS THAT OVER 2,000 YEARS AGO, THE PASS WAS FORTIFIED. ACCORDING TO ANCIENT ACCOUNTS, ALEXANDER THE GREAT BUILT IRON GATES IN THE CAUCASUS TO KEEP THE UNCIVILIZED BARBARIANS TO THE NORTH FROM INVADING THE SOUTH. SOME HISTORIANS THINK THE STORY OF ALEXANDER'S BARRIER PROBABLY DESCRIBED THE DARIAL PASS.

The Alans became wealthy from taxing any merchants traveling through the Darial Pass.

By the Middle Ages, Alania was a small kingdom surrounded by far larger neighbors. Alania was important, however. It controlled the Darial Pass, which was part of the Silk Road. This was the main trade route by which goods from South and East Asia reached Europe. Trade made Alania wealthy.

A BRIEF HISTORY

In the 800s, the Alans formed an alliance with their more powerful northern neighbor, the Khazars. In the early 900s, the Alans came under the influence of the growing Byzantine Empire based in Constantinople (modern-day Istanbul, in Turkey). This new influence might reflect the fact that the Alan leader had converted to Christianity.

North Ossetia has many ancient Orthodox, or traditional, Christian churches and monasteries, like this one.

This delicately patterned silk was imported to Europe from Central Asia along the Silk Road.

THE SILK ROUTE

THE DARIAL PASS WAS A KEY PART OF THE SILK ROAD. FOR MORE THAN 1,500 YEARS FROM AROUND 120 BC UNTIL AD 1450, THE SILK ROUTE WAS THE MAIN OVERLAND ROUTE FROM CHINA TO THE WEST. THE SILK ROUTE WAS ACTUALLY A NUMBER OF TRADE ROUTES THAT CROSSED THOUSANDS OF MILES OF DESERTS, MOUNTAINS, PLAINS, AND SEAS. ITS NAME CAME FROM SILK, WHICH THE CHINESE INVENTED AND WHICH WAS HIGHLY PRIZED IN THE WEST. SILK WAS NOT THE ONLY MERCHANDISE TRADED ALONG THE ROUTE, HOWEVER. **CARAVANS** FROM ASIA ALSO CARRIED SPICES, PRECIOUS METALS, FOODS, IVORY, AND OTHER FABRICS TO THE WEST.

THE FOUNDING OF RUSSIA

KIEVAN RUS' EMERGED IN THE LATE 800s AS A POWER IN WHAT IS NOW RUSSIA WITH A CAPITAL AT NOVGOROD. ACCORDING TO STORIES OF THE TIME, A LEADER NAMED RURIK AND HIS BROTHERS WERE INVITED TO LEAD THE EASTERN SLAVS WHO LIVED IN THE REGION. RURIK WAS FROM A VARANGIAN TRIBE NAMED THE RUS. THE VARANGIANS WERE VIKINGS FROM SCANDINAVIA. RURIK'S SUCCESSORS LATER MOVED THE CAPITAL TO KIEV, IN WHAT IS NOW UKRAINE. THE KIEVAN RUS' EMPIRE REACHED ITS GREATEST EXTENT IN THE MID-1000s, BUT THEN BEGAN TO DECLINE. IN THE 1240s IT WAS OVERTHROWN BY THE MONGOLS. RURIK'S DESCENDANTS LATER RULED MOSCOW AND WERE CZARS OF RUSSIA UNTIL THE 1600s.

Vikings used their longboats to sail along Russia's rivers as they opened new trade routes.

In the 900s, Constantinople was the center of the Eastern Orthodox Church. This was a form of Christianity that had grown separately from the Roman Catholic Church of Europe. An Arab traveler to the Caucasus wrote of the Alans, "Their king is Christian at heart but all his people are **idolaters**."

A SERIES OF WARS

In the 920s, the Byzantines went to war against the Khazars. During the conflict, the Byzantines defeated Alania. The Alans abandoned Christianity and followed neighboring peoples in adopting Islam. The Alans again aligned themselves with the Khazars until about 960, when the Khazar kingdom was defeated by invaders from Kievan Rus' and collapsed.

In need of protection, the Alans formed alliances with a number of peoples, particularly the Byzantines and the Georgians. These allies helped the Alans fight off attacks from aggressive northern tribes.

Genghis Khan led his Mongol forces into the Caucasus in 1238. The Alans fell under Mongol rule for a century.

In this painting from the early 1900s, the Rus prepare to burn the body of a dead noble in a Viking ship. It was believed that the ship would take the dead person to the afterlife.

The Alans also formed trading partnerships with different tribes, including the Rus who came from the north. The Rus had founded Kievan Rus' in 862. In 988 they had adopted Christianity from the Byzantine Empire. Later, the Rus would expand their territory to found modern-day Russia.

In 1238 Mongols led by Genghis Khan invaded Alania. The Mongols had defeated the Alans' allies in Georgia. The brutality of the invaders drove some Alans into the mountains.

THE MONGOL EMPIRE

DURING THE 1200s, MONGOL LEADERS DEFEATED ENEMY AFTER ENEMY TO CREATE THE LARGEST EMPIRE THE WORLD HAD THEN SEEN. THE FIRST MONGOL LEADER, GENGHIS KHAN, BROUGHT TOGETHER NOMADIC PEOPLE FROM THE STEPPES OF CENTRAL ASIA UNDER HIS RULE IN 1206. THE MONGOLS WERE SKILLED HORSEMEN AND FOUGHT ON HORSEBACK WITH BOWS AND ARROWS. A COMBINATION OF WARFARE AND TRADE HELPED GENGHIS KHAN AND HIS DESCENDANTS GROW THE EMPIRE QUICKLY. BY THE LATE 1200s THE MONGOLS RULED AN AREA THAT STRETCHED FROM CENTRAL EUROPE EAST TO CHINA AND THE SEA OF JAPAN AND SOUTH INTO THE INDIAN SUBCONTINENT. IN THE 1300s, THE EMPIRE FELL APART AS QUICKLY AS IT HAD GROWN AS MONGOL LEADERS FOUGHT CIVIL WARS TO TRY TO GAIN POWER.

The Mongols were skilled warriors who defeated Chinese and Islamic armies as they built their empire.

21

The Mongols absorbed the Alans into the Mongol Empire. The Alans found themselves forced to fight in Mongol armies. They took part in Mongol campaigns from Europe to southern China. The Mongols organized the Alans into their own units. Around 30,000 Alans formed the royal guard at the Yuan court in Beijing, China. The Alans were loyal servants to the Chinese royal court until the middle of the 1300s.

THE END OF ALANIA

Alania came to an end in the late 1300s. Another Mongol invader, Timur, destroyed what little remained of the kingdom. The Alans split into three groups. Two of these groups, which were known as the Digor and the Iron, made their homes in the foothills and valleys of the Caucasus Mountains. The third group moved west into eastern Europe.

The Mongols forced conquered peoples such as the Alans to fight in their armies.

The Ossetians, like these men photographed in traditional dress in the 1920s, are the descendants of the Alans.

Experts believe it was probably the Alans or their descendants who built the City of the Dead in the 1100s or 1500s. There is little direct evidence to prove this, but the Alans lived in the region when the huts were probably built. That makes the Alans the likely builders. Until it is possible to carry out more archaeological investigation at the site, this remains the widely accepted **theory**.

The Caucasus came under the control of the Soviet Union in the 1920s. After the Soviet Union broke up in 1991, the Caucasus became a series of small republics, including North Ossetia. In November 1994, in recognition of the past role of the Alans, North Ossetia was officially renamed North Ossetia–Alania.

SECRETS OF THE PAST

The City of the Dead is surrounded by mysteries. No one knows if they will ever be solved. Many local stories have been passed down over the centuries about the site. People in the region tell different accounts of the city and why it was abandoned. One legend says that anyone who dares to enter the village will never be able to leave. Local people say that is the reason they never visit the city on the hill.

Another legend says that the city marks where warriors once kidnapped a beautiful woman from beyond the valley.

Local people never step inside the low stone wall that marks the boundary of the City of the Dead.

Do tales passed down through generations of Ossetians hold clues about the building of the huts?

It is said warriors quarrelled about who owned the woman. When they could not decide, they killed her. The gods were angry with the warriors and punished them by striking them down with disease. The warriors died in the huts. According to the legend, it is their bones that lie in the crypts.

MYSTERIOUS BOATS

Some of the bodies inside the huts have been found lying in wooden structures that look like canoes. One boat even had what seems to be an oar next to it. Archaeologists have no idea why people might have been buried in boats. None of the nearby rivers were suitable for navigation by boat.

One explanation could be that the people were following funeral customs seen among a number of ancient peoples.

Some of the remains at Dargavs were found in simple wooden canoes hollowed out of logs.

The ancient Egyptians, Mesopotamians, and Greeks all believed that a dead person had to cross a river to get to the **afterlife**. Another theory about the canoes is that the boats in the crypts are related to the Vikings. The Vikings of Scandinavia buried their dead in boats. The Vikings later moved to Rus. Perhaps their beliefs somehow made their way to the Caucasus.

LUCKY COINS

Another unanswered question is why each hut has a well in front of it. People visiting the site have found coins next to the huts. Experts believe that when the ancient Ossetians or Alans died and were placed in the crypts, their relatives threw a coin into the well. If the coin reached the bottom of the well, it was a sign that the soul of the dead person had reached heaven.

ANCIENT EGYPTIAN AFTERLIFE

THE ANCIENT EGYPTIANS BELIEVED THAT A DEAD PERSON ONLY REACHED THE AFTERLIFE IF CERTAIN RITES WERE FOLLOWED AFTER HIS OR HER DEATH. THE RITES INCLUDED PRESERVING THE BODY THROUGH MUMMIFICATION. THE BODY WAS BURIED WITH ALL THE GOODS THE PERSON NEEDED FOR THE NEXT LIFE, INCLUDING FOOD, SLAVES, AND VALUED POSSESSIONS. THE JOURNEY TO THE AFTERLIFE ALSO INVOLVED A TRIP ALONG THE RIVER NILE. THE ANCIENT EGYPTIANS BELIEVED THAT THE DEAD USED THE RIVER AS WELL AS THE LIVING. THEY OFTEN BURIED A MODEL BOAT WITH THE DEAD PERSON. THIS PART OF THEIR FUNERAL PRACTICES IS ECHOED IN THE USE OF CANOE-LIKE BOATS TO HOLD THE DEAD AT DARGAVS.

The Egyptians held elaborate rituals to help a dead person reach the afterlife, as shown in this depiction of an Egyptian king's funeral.

The Vikings burned their dead in ships or sometimes buried the whole ship in a mound-shaped tomb.

Whenever a person visited his or her family's crypt, they checked whether their relative had reached heaven by throwing a coin down the well. Experts believe this might explain why coins have been found around the entrances to the huts.

ISOLATION HUTS

There is another theory about what happened to the people in the City of the Dead. Some historians believe that a **plague** swept through the area some time between the 1500s and the 1700s. The death rate was so high that the population fell steeply. From a maximum of about 200,000 people in the area, just 16,000 people were left by the 1800s.

The story about the plague fits with local stories that people entered the huts when they were alive. Some experts think that any family suspected of having the plague was sent to the huts to avoid **contaminating** their neighbors.

BOATS AND DEATH

THE EGYPTIANS WERE NOT THE ONLY ANCIENT PEOPLE WHO LINKED DEATH, WATER, AND BOATS. IN ANCIENT MESOPOTAMIA, PEOPLE BELIEVED THAT ANY BODY OF WATER COULD CARRY A DEAD PERSON TO THE NEXT LIFE. IN ANCIENT GREECE, A MYTH TOLD HOW A BOATMAN NAMED CHARON WOULD FERRY A DEAD PERSON ACROSS THE RIVER STYX TO THE NEXT LIFE. THE DEAD WERE BURIED WITH COINS TO PAY CHARON. IN VIKING CULTURE, THE MOST IMPORTANT AND WEALTHY PEOPLE WERE PLACED IN A BOAT AND SAILED OUT TO SEA OR BURIED. THE TOMBS OF OTHER VIKINGS WERE SURROUNDED BY BOAT SHAPES MADE FROM STANDING STONES.

This painting from the late 1800s illustrates the Greek myth in which Charon ferries the souls of the dead across the River Styx.

29

Did people move into the huts when they got sick? Some experts believe whole families were condemned to die there.

Whole families suspected of having the plague might have been moved into the huts with supplies of food. If they survived the plague, they would have starved to death when their food ran out. Infected people who did not have any family members to care for them would have waited for death in the large **communal** crypt.

Archaeologists are not all sure about the plague theory. A body in one hut was wrapped in cloth after death. This is unlikely to have been done if the person died from plague, because no one would touch the body. The theory could easily be tested if archaeologists were able to work at the site today. They could use modern technology to test the bones to see what had killed the person.

WATCHING OVER THE DEAD

A tall, stone watchtower overlooks the City of the Dead. Experts believe that in the ancient Ossetian–Alanian culture, a burial site always had a tower to guard the dead. Today the watchtower is damaged. Its top is open and archaeologists do not know what kind of roof, if any, it originally had. There is an entrance into the tower, but it is only accessible by ladder. At the top of the tower are what seem to be ornamental balconies. No one knows what they were used for. The watchtower also stands slightly away from the crypts just inside the surrounding perimeter wall. No one knows who built the low stone wall. Archaeologists believe that it was most likely built at the same time as the crypts. It may have been intended to mark the limits of the site.

Inside the tower, a series of wooden ladders lead to the top. What were the occupants using the lookout for?

31

The tombs are built from stone blocks covered with a smooth layer of light-colored plaster.

IS THE CITY OF THE DEAD UNIQUE?

The City of the Dead at Dargavs is not the only collection of crypts in the Caucasus region, although it is the most impressive. It has some features in common with another necropolis called Tsoi-Pede in modern-day Chechnya.

Tsoi-Pede was built by the Nakh people of the northern Caucasus. Some experts wonder whether the Nakh people might have also built Dargavs, rather than the Ossetian-Alanian people. One of the key features of Nakh architecture is the tower. The Nakh used towers for military purposes as well as for houses. The peak period of Nakh tower building was between the 1400s and the 1600s. Another typical feature of Nakh architecture is a curved, ridged roof. Again, this is a feature that occurs at the City of the Dead in Dargavs.

THE HOME OF THE GODS

TSOI-PEDE IS A **NECROPOLIS** IN THE ITUM-KALI REGION OF PRESENT-DAY CHECHNYA, ANOTHER REPUBLIC IN THE CAUCASUS. ITS NAME MEANS "THE HOME OF THE GODS." LIKE THE CITY OF THE DEAD AT DARGAVS, IT HAS CRYPTS AND TOMBS BUILT CLOSE TO EACH OTHER ON A HILL. THERE ARE 42 TOMBS IN ALL. A WATCHTOWER OVERLOOKS THE SITE FROM THE TOP OF THE HILL. ARCHAEOLOGISTS BELIEVE THAT TSOI-PEDE WAS BUILT IN THE MIDDLE AGES, POSSIBLY IN THE 1400s.

The necropolis at Tsoi-Pede is one of the most popular tourist sites in the Republic of Chechnya.

INVESTIGATING THE PAST

There is still a lot to learn about Russia's City of the Dead. The remote location and the unstable political situation in the region mean the site has been largely ignored by modern archaeologists. From what they know already, however, historians have been able to come up with a theory.

Did the stone wall that surrounds the site act as a boundary to keep the sick people inside under quarantine?

The City of the Dead is a difficult drive from the North Ossetian capital at Vladikavkaz.

Historical evidence shows that the region suffered a huge loss of population sometime between the early 1500s and the early 1800s. The population was almost wiped out. The most likely causes for such a decline are warfare or disease. There is no record of wars at the time, so disease is the most likely cause.

Most modern experts believe that the city was used as a **quarantine** site when plague hit the region. Whole families and their children probably moved into the huts — and never came out again. Neighbors may have left food near the wall around the city for the people inside. Many local people still refuse to visit the City of the Dead today. This might be because of different stories about the plague.

ARCHAEOLOGICAL INVESTIGATIONS

The Soviet Union broke up in 1991. Since then, there has been political unrest as the different republics in the Caucasus region fight for independence from Russia. As a result, the area is too dangerous for archaeologists to carry out lengthy excavations. At the moment, there is no archaeological work being done at the City of the Dead.

The journey from North Ossetia's capital city of Vladikavkaz to Dargavs takes between one and three hours. The road is winding and dangerous as it travels through mountain passes. The site is high up in the mountains. The weather there is often misty and foggy, which makes traveling to the site even more hazardous.

SOVIET TOURISM

BEFORE THE COLLAPSE OF THE SOVIET UNION IN 1991, DARGAVS WAS A POPULAR DESTINATION FOR TOURISTS. BUSLOADS OF TOURISTS MADE THE LONG AND DIFFICULT JOURNEY TO SEE THE CRYPTS. THERE WAS AN OFFICE AT THE SITE, WHERE A LOCAL WOMAN SOLD ENTRANCE TICKETS. LOCAL PEOPLE ALSO OPENED OTHER TOURIST FACILITIES TO PROVIDE VISITORS WITH FOOD AND DRINK. HOWEVER, FEW PEOPLE FROM OUTSIDE THE SOVIET UNION VISITED, WHICH IS ONE REASON WHY ARCHAEOLOGISTS KNOW SO LITTLE ABOUT THE SITE TODAY.

Soviet tourists visit Dargavs in 1964. Very few tourists visit the site today.

The Aymara people who lived in Peru before the Inca used burial towers as tombs for their dead.

When the Soviet Union broke up in 1991, Dargavs became part of North Ossetia. Tourists need special permits to visit Dargavs. The permits are not always granted. Anyone visiting the site without a permit risks being thrown out of the country. For people who make it to Dargavs, there is nowhere to stay. Only the boldest tourists make the trip. They say that the City of the Dead has a unique atmosphere. Many find the fact that so many bodies lie exposed upsetting. Up to 10,000 people are said to be buried there, although there is no way to confirm the figure.

The remains of other similar crypts are dotted across the region. These cities of the dead are not unique to the Caucasus. Almost 2,000 years ago, **funerary** towers were built at Palmyra in present-day Syria. In Peru, the Aymara people built funeral towers before the Inca came to dominate the area.

FUNERARY TOWERS IN PALMYRA

PALMYRA IS AN ANCIENT ROMAN SITE IN THE DESERTS OF SYRIA, IN THE MIDDLE EAST. THE SITE WAS HOME TO A NUMBER OF STONE FUNERARY TOWERS THAT IN SOME WAYS RESEMBLE THE STONE TOWERS OF THE CAUCASUS. THE TOWERS AT PALMYRA DATE FROM THE 100s AD. WEALTHY FAMILIES BUILT THE MULTISTORY SANDSTONE TOWERS TO HOUSE THE COFFINS, OR SARCOPHAGUSES, OF DEAD FAMILY MEMBERS. SOME OF THE TOWERS COULD HOLD AS MANY AS 300 SARCOPHAGUSES. IN 2015, THE TERRORIST GROUP KNOWN AS ISLAMIC STATE DESTROYED SOME OF THE TOWERS.

Wealthy families built towers with a series of floors to hold the coffins of relatives that died.

WHAT CAN MUMMIES TEACH US?

IT IS FRUSTRATING FOR ARCHAEOLOGISTS THAT THEY CANNOT EXAMINE THE MUMMIES AT DARGAVS. MUMMIES CAN TELL EXPERTS ALL SORTS OF INFORMATION, INCLUDING WHETHER THEY WERE MALE OR FEMALE, OR YOUNG OR OLD. EXPERTS CAN LEARN WHAT THE PERSON ATE, HOW THEY LIVED, AND HOW THEY DIED. SCIENTISTS MAY BE ABLE TO TELL FROM THE MUMMIES' CLOTHING WHAT THEIR SOCIAL POSITION WAS IN THEIR COMMUNITY. MODERN TECHNOLOGY USES DNA PROFILING. THAT ALLOWS ARCHAEOLOGISTS TO FIGURE OUT A MUMMY'S ANCESTRY. AT DARGAVS, THAT WOULD REVEAL WHETHER THE DEAD WERE ALANS OR IF THEY BELONGED TO A DIFFERENT GROUP.

An archaeologist prepares to examine an ancient child mummy from Peru. Scans of the mummy's bones will reveal information about the child's life.

There are numerous ruined medieval villages in North Ossetia. Were the people who lived there the people who built the City of the Dead?

MUMMIFICATION

Existing photographs of the City of the Dead show that some of the bodies have mummified over time. The cold dry climate has dried and preserved the bodies. Once archaeologists can study the site, they will use the latest technology to determine the age of the mummies and how they died.

Archaeologists have discovered mummies in South America that are more than 6,000 years old. The mummies of Dargavs are thought to be far younger. Experts are confident from what they know about the site that the bodies there are no more than 1,000 years old — and they may be as "young"

WHAT RELIGION WERE THE PEOPLE AT DARGAVS?

In the 1600s, Islamic invaders conquered the Caucasus. Many people there converted to Islam. In the distant past, the Ossetians had followed a **pagan** belief system. In the 1200s the Alans had been Eastern Orthodox Christians under the Byzantine Empire. When Ossetia was absorbed into the Russian Empire in 1774, the Ossetian-Alans did not completely embrace Orthodox Christianity, which was the state religion. They continued to practice their own blend of religions.

Today, it is difficult to say precisely which religion the dead at Dargavs followed.

This mosque stands in Vladikavkaz. Many modern Ossetians follow Islam, though others remain Christian.

The huts will only reveal their secrets when archaeologists can safely visit the site and examine the remains.

It is known that the Ossetians' religion blended aspects of Christianity with folk beliefs. This included traditional rituals such as **sacrificing** animals and praying to their own saints. The Ossetians also built **shrines**, but we do not know who they worshiped.

Today, many Ossetians do not consider themselves to be Christian. According to the latest Russian **census** of 2012, almost one third of Ossetians claim to practice their own **ethnic** religion. Perhaps the dead of the hillside city practiced a similar religion? Like so much about the site, we do not know. We can only wait until archaeologists are able to reach the City of the Dead and begin to solve its many mysteries.

TIMELINE

AD

72   The Alans are recorded as living near the Darial Pass in the Caucasus.

800s   The Alans make an alliance with their more powerful neighbors, the Khazars.

900s   Early in the century, an Alan king adopts Christianity from the Byzantine Empire.

920s   Alania is defeated by the Byzantines during a Byzantine war against the Khazars.

988   The Rus of Kievan Rus' adopt Christianity.

1100s   This is the earliest date that has been suggested for the building of the first crypts at Dargavs.

1238   Mongols invade and conquer Alania, forcing its men to serve in Mongol armies.

1300s   Alania ceases to exist as an independent kingdom late in the 1300s.

1400s   The Nakh people of the Caucasus begin their own tradition of building funerary towers.

1450   The Silk Road, the overland trade route from China to the West, begins to lose its importance.

1500s	This is the most popular estimate of when the huts at Dargavs were first built.
	An epidemic of plague strikes the Caucasus at about this time. The population falls steeply over the next two centuries.
1600s	Islamic invaders take over much of the Caucasus. Many peoples there adopt Islam as their faith.
1700s	The plague causes the population in North Ossetia to fall from around 200,000 at the start of the century to only 16,000 at its end.
1774	Ossetia becomes part of the Russian Empire.
1830	Local tradition says that the last hut at Dargavs was built around now.
1920s	Ossetia becomes part of the Soviet Union.
1991	The Soviet Union breaks up. North Ossetia becomes an independent republic.
1994	North Ossetia is officially renamed North Ossetia–Alania.

GLOSSARY

afterlife Life after death.

archaeologists People who study history by examining old structures and artifacts.

caravans Large groups of merchants and their animals traveling together.

census An official count of the number of people who live in a country.

communal Describes something shared by a community.

contaminating Spread disease from one person to another.

corpses Dead bodies.

crypt A room used as a burial place, often underground.

ethnic Relating to a small group living within a larger population.

excavated Dug up and recorded in a methodical way.

funerary Relating to a funeral or the commemoration of the dead.

groin vaults An arched vault formed when two round-shaped ceilings intersect.

idolaters People who worship images of gods, known as idols.

mortar A mixture of cement, sand, and water used in construction.

mummified Describes a body that has been preserved by becoming dried out.

necropolis A cemetery, usually belonging to an ancient city.

nomadic Moving around, with no permanent home.

pagan Describes religious beliefs that do not belong to the world's major religions.

pitch The angle at which a roof slopes.

plague A serious disease that spreads easily and causes fever and often death.

quarantine A place where people who may have a disease are kept in isolation so they cannot pass it on.

republic A government in which power is held by the people and their elected leaders.

sacrificing Killing a person or animal or giving up a valued possession to honor a god.

shrines Buildings marking places that are thought to be divine.

theory An explanation of something that fits the evidence but which has not been proved.

FURTHER INFORMATION

Books

Coene, Frederik.
The Caucasus: An Introduction (Routledge Contemporary Russia and Eastern Europe). New York: Routledge, 2011.

McCray, Thomas.
Russia and the Former Soviet Republics. (Modern World Cultures). New York: Chelsea House Publishers, 2006.

Roudik, Peter L.
Culture and Customs of the Caucasus (Cultures and Customs of the World). Westport, Conn: Greenwood, 2008.

Websites

http://www.atlasobscura. com/places/dargavs-village -city-of-the-dead
An article about the City of the Dead, with photographs.

http://academickids.com/ encyclopedia/index.php/ Caucasus
An encyclopedia page about the history and geography of the Caucasus region

wiki.kidzsearch.com/wiki/ North_Ossetia-Alania
A page for kids about North Ossetia–Alania, with a map.

INDEX